A Bigfoot Bestiary and Other Wonders

Newsflash! Bigfoot has been found! He resides in the mind of Martin Achatz who rides with "love as big as Kong" this doppelgänger of a beast straight into the mystery that is his own life. And with abundant humor as well—Bigfoot has late fees at the Carnegie Library, goes trick-or-treating, auditions for Picasso to replace the Minotaur.

—Dennis Hinrichsen,
author of *Dominion + Selected Poems*

Wade into Martin Achatz's new book and you will feel a strange, wonderful undertow. Let it take you. This is a beguiling love story about Bigfoot and about more than Bigfoot. These poems welcome mystery, cradle sadness, and remind us how deliciously inventive language can feel.

—Cindy Hunter Morgan,
author of *Harborless* and *Far Company*

Martin Achatz knows what it is to be big and hairy and to express the animal inside us. To paraphrase the Zen koan, live as if you were already Bigfoot. If Iowa Poet Laureate Marvin Bell has his *Dead Man* poems, Michigan's Achatz has rendered poetical the great ape of the Northwoods, and he eloquently and determinedly immerses us in the dream, meanwhile paying homage to Robert Frost, Pablo Neruda, Wallace Stevens, Flannery O'Connor, and all the other wonderful monsters.

—Bonnie Jo Campbell,
author of *The Waters* and *American Salvage*

Martin Achatz reimagines the legendary Bigfoot in his newest book, a funny and moving collection of poems that is playfully serious. Achatz melds cryptozoologic wonder with the heartrending stuff of the everyday world ... a fierce Sasquatch howl that illuminates and reveals the fragile state of our collective humanity.

—W. Todd Kaneko,
author of *This Is How the Bone Sings*

A BIGFOOT BESTIARY
AND OTHER WONDERS

ALSO BY THE AUTHOR

The Mysteries of the Rosary

A BIGFOOT BESTIARY AND OTHER WONDERS

Martin Achatz

Modern History Press
Ann Arbor, MI

Library of Congress Cataloging-in-Publication Data

Names: Achatz, Martin, 1967- author.
Title: A bigfoot bestiary and other wonders : poems / Martin Achatz.
Description: Ann Arbor, MI : Modern History Press, 2024. | Summary: "The
    Bigfoot poetry cycle examines the foibles and follies of the human race
    through a wise, external observer in the form of the mythical monster
    Bigfoot. Through his alien eyes, we gain a better sense of what it is to
    be human"-- Provided by publisher.
Identifiers: LCCN 2024037162 (print) | LCCN 2024037163 (ebook) | ISBN
    9781615998340 (trade paperback) | ISBN 9781615998357 (hardcover) | ISBN
    9781615998364 (epub)
Subjects: LCSH: Sasquatch--Poetry. | LCGFT: Poetry.
Classification: LCC PS3601.C5 B54 2024 (print) | LCC PS3601.C5 (ebook) |
    DDC 811/.6--dc23/eng/20240820
LC record available at https://lccn.loc.gov/2024037162
LC ebook record available at https://lccn.loc.gov/2024037163

Book #1 in the Yooper Poetry Series

ISBN 978-1-61599-834-0 paperback
ISBN 978-1-61599-835-7 hardcover
ISBN 978-1-61599-836-4 eBook

Cover design by Mona Z. Kraculdy
Cover image by Amelia Pruiett
Flipbook animation by Lukman Inkstoon

Published by
Modern History Press   www.ModernHistoryPress.com
5145 Pontiac Trail   info@ModernHistoryPress.com
Ann Arbor, MI 48105   Toll-free 888-761-6268

Distributed by Ingram Group (USA/CAN/AU/EU)

Audiobook available from Audible.com and iTunes

for Celeste and Gideon,
the two greatest wonders of my life

Contents

Tall and Hairy

TALL AND HAIRY

"There were giants on the earth in those days, and also afterward, when the sons of God came in to the daughters of men and they bore children to them. Those were the mighty men who were of old, men of renown."
    —Genesis 6:4 NKJV

"I think to have an element of mystery in life is very, very important."
    —Dr. Jane Goodall

A Question About Bigfoot

Do I believe in Bigfoot?
That's not easy to answer.
It's like trying to figure out
love after 25 years of marriage.
Does my wife still love me?
Do I still love her?
Will she meet someone
in the dairy section at Walmart
as they both reach for the same
half gallon of 1% milk,
in a second lose the ineffable,
what's bound us to each other
like a filament from a spider's
spinneret? What sets love
in motion then lights it on fire
until it burns down like
a lit bottle rocket?
What I'm talking about
here is mystery. I want to
believe in Bigfoot, that love
won't fuse out, shoot into
heaven, be gone faster
than a startled rabbit. Because
really, what's life without
mysteries? Just a half gallon
of 1% milk, curdled, separated
in the back of the fridge.

The Eighth Day, a Bigfoot Creation Story

After God had taken a nap,
He looked around at everything
He'd made. All the four-legged,
two-legged, hairy, and scaled.
The giraffe with its punchline
neck. Blue whales as big
as His thumbs. Bald eagles, cardinals,
jays diving, circling the heavens
of His nostrils. And man and woman,
shivering, stupid with curiosity.

God saw that His work
wasn't done, so He reached down,
gathered redwood sapling,
rhino tusk, mammoth hair.
Folded in magma and ice shag,
the roar of asteroid dust. Borrowed
milk from the woman.
Mixed these ingredients,
molded them into something
that was so much like Him
He almost smashed it to fossil.

But instead, He leaned down, coughed
life into its lungs, told it to go
forth, hide in cave, Himalaya.
Haunt the border,
stay blurry,
lumber
alone.

Thirteen Ways of Looking at Bigfoot

I.

In the pines along U.S. 41,
Bigfoot stitches the afternoon
dark then bright then dark again.

II.

Salmon run
in the Dead River.
Upstream, Bigfoot waits,
hungry for silver spawn.

III.

The fat kid on the playground
has a mind of Bigfoot,
a deep chromosomal urge
to hide under the monkey bars.

IV.

Bigfoot does not have patience.
He eats the sweetest blueberry
before the grubs and pinecones,
reads the last page
of the mystery first.

V.

Blackbirds dance
in the green air.

Bigfoot hurls stones
up and up, reverse
Perseids through
the feathered ballet.

   VI.

If you meet Bigfoot
hiking in the mountains,
don't stare at his feet.

   VII.

Bob Dylan's singing
makes Bigfoot miss
his mother's lullabies.

   VIII.

The smell of skunk
in the middle of the night.
Bigfoot must be moving.

   IX.

After the rains,
there are footprints
up and down the riverbank,
Bigfoot still searching
for the goddamn ark
before the flood.

     a bigfoot bestiary and other wonders

X.

On a foggy evening,
it's easy to mistake
Bigfoot for God
strolling through Eden.

XI.

Bigfoot and a Syrian refugee
walk into a bar.
The bartender looks
at the refugee, says,
"We don't serve your kind in here,"
breaking Bigfoot's immigrant heart.

XII.

Bigfoot once fell in love
with a black bear, loved
how she clawed his back
the way Callisto claws the stars.

XIII.

I saw Bigfoot
walking down the street
one morning. He reminded
me of my dead brother
out for his morning smoke.

Bigfoot's Heart

for Lee LaForge

How do you measure it, a love as big
as Kong, hungry for Fay Wray's sparrow breasts
and silent-movie eyes, her screams that dig
into feral chambers of his ape chest,

take root, blossom on that island of bones?
Or Karloff, staring through lizard lids, his bride
full of lightning and terror, her soft moans
stirring his anvil of blood, while outside

peasants howl? Follow footprints on the shores
of Gichigami, prehistoric leaps
in the sucking sands, listen for the roars
of all the brokenhearted, as tide creeps

to your ankles. Count the waves, their hisses
filling night with breath and tongue and kisses.

Bigfoot Hungers

All Bigfoots crave dead eel,
fennel, ginger heeled in jicama,
krill, lamprey—marinated not oiled—
pancaked quail, ribbed salmon that ulcerates,
veined worms, xanthic yams,
zwiebacked zucchini.

Field Guide for the North American Bigfoot

after Wisława Szymborska

Look where green is endless, night always
full lunar eclipse. If you see black bear
or deer or skunk, the gold of ruffled grouse
in pine or spruce, you're in the wrong place.

Bigfoot prefers to be Garbo, photographed
from behind or in a blur of flight, in dark glasses,
scarf turbaned about his head.

Despite his obviousness, Bigfoot is
difficult to pick out in a lineup of oak or maple,
as if he's always turning color, shedding leaves,
ready to bud into full summer.

Bigfoot calls don't work.
His number is unlisted.

You might think you smell Bigfoot
by the compost pile, but it could be
cabbage or eggshells or used teabags,
maybe trout scales from yesterday's catch
that flash like quartz in the sun.

You can lure Bigfoot with ice cream and Netflix.
Let him watch *Breaking Bad* while polishing
off a quart of Chunky Monkey.

We don't like mystery anywhere,
would rather dissect Houdini's brain
to figure out how he made an elephant
disappear like Bigfoot in morning mist.

Bigfoot is an endangered species
in Russia, France, and Germany
because "a society that forgets art

risks losing its soul" according
to Camille Paglia.

If you want to find Bigfoot,
just stop looking.

The Missing

Roger and Bob rode quarter horses, one named Chico, up and down that wrecked creek bed, searching for something they didn't know was missing. At night, they camped under feedbags of stars, ate canned beans, maybe peaches, spoke baritone secrets, the way parents talk in tangled blankets after midnight about sons who've started making sounds like hungry macaques behind locked bathroom doors. Roger and Bob slept close to each other for warmth, the press of skin in cold October jack pines.

On day 20, rounding a crow's nest of roots, they finally found what they were looking for. Crouched by the running stream, Bob reached for his rifle. Roger grabbed his camera, began to film.

Lady Bigfoot stood, loped toward the tree line, her orangutan arms and breasts, sidelong glance, sequoia torso slid into Six Rivers Forest with all the missing. Roger, who would be dead in a few years from cancer. Bob, who wouldn't speak about Roger for decades. Chico, who was buried in a drainage ditch with a cow.

Now they're just stuttering home movies played over and over, backward, forward, at family gatherings after the potato salad has been eaten and everyone tries to remember the name of the other horse. Was it Buckwheat? Mel? Graynose or Featherhead? *It was Sassy*, insists one cousin, *because she bucked and bit, ended up getting a bullet between the eyes.*

Bigfoot Shadows

A shadow looms, something you half-
recognize. Deer? Coyote? Your uncle's
shade that went into his basement
one afternoon with a shotgun?
It's larger, a black hole with legs
that blots out everything—
sycamore, feral swine,
lakes scooped out by glaciers,
hunger for meatloaf your mother
no longer knows how to make,
hamburger and egg and oatmeal
kneaded together, folded into
a bread pan, nestled deep
in the oven behind her
eyes.

You aim your Subaru down
U.S. 41. Headlights stitch
night with comet tails, carve
shapes into dark constellations—
a pine stump you fell on as a kid,
yellow jackets oiling across
your back. The shoulders, arms
of your junior prom date whose
skin made your fingers sing
"*Nessun dorma*" in the backseat.
Your sister who died one August
morning when breath became ripple
then wave then tide then lake
then ocean then horizon then Venus
then Milky Way then
nothing.

You must decide
whether to brake, slow down,
stop. Let the umbra cross

the road before you, a dark
mammoth. Or speed up, continue on,
hope it slips back into the woods
like a fog of flushed partridges,
or a loon ghost echoing, echoing
over a dusky pond forever. The way
the smell of Kools and Seven Crown
lingered on and on after
your dad kissed you
goodnight.

Bigfoot Visits My Father's Grave

Can I tell you I see him
most nights, sitting beside the stone,
thick fingers pressed into the ridges
of my father's name, as if petting
marble ants or grubs?
That my father's bones
call him, flood the empty
catacombs of his chest
with longing, like the rasp
of reindeer moss longs
for a dermis of snow?
He rocks where deer graze
among Virgins, saints, silk roses.
Ruby eternal flames wink
like traffic lights, caution
living and dead
to slow, pause, idle
at this intersection
between breath and beyond.

I wonder what fish
breeches the ocean surface
in his skull, if he's hunched
at the mouth of the Chocolay
with his dad again, the old man's hoary
back ridged with knuckles
of vertebrae as he teaches his son
how to sink his hand in water,
wait until a fat white belly
glides into his palm. Then the dragonfly
snatch, the stunned slap of silver
on rock and sand, as if still trying to climb
upstream to spawn. This is
his feral elegy, peeling meat
from bone, burying the filigree
of ribs in pine roots, venerating

the migration of geese, cycle of blueberry,
crabapple, first frost on October cattails.

Loss is hieroglyph
to him, like the letters
beneath his raisin fingertips:
F. R. E. D.
These curves and lines fill him
with wonder, fear. As if the moon
is walking the tree line behind him,
leaving bright footprints
in the needles and ferns.

Bigfoot and Jim Harrison Skinny-Dip in Morgan Pond on Father's Day

for Kathleen H.

They look like father and son as they wade into the shallows, Bigfoot three feet taller than Harrison and smelling like bear scat. Harrison smells of Dewar's and onion, and the crescents of his buttocks glow in the dusk like swans. The clay sucks at their shins as they move deeper, shadows of perch and rainbow darting away in startled splash and foam. Bigfoot keeps his eyes on Harrison, who has already fallen once on shore, tripping as he shed his pants and underwear. Bigfoot lays a hairy arm across Harrison's shoulders, leaves it there the way a moose might shelter a calf under its haunches during a thunderstorm. Harrison listens to the peepers drill the night with music, and he starts to hum, then sings, "And the cat's in the cradle and the silver spoon." He holds onto the last word, draws it out like a wolf howl. Bigfoot pushes his thick tongue to the roof of his mouth and coughs like a coyote in duet. Harrison is up to his nipples in water now, and he raises his one good eye to Bigfoot and croons, "Little boy blue and the man in the moon." His voice is full of booze and cigarettes, like logs in a flood. Bigfoot can't help himself, reaches down and scoops the writer up like a baby, rocks him back and forth, back and forth. Bigfoot knows the hunger of loss, has chased it through canyon and forest until the trees of his legs were weak as saplings. Harrison presses his head against Bigfoot's chest and sobs.

Bigfoot strokes Harrison's Buddha belly, purrs into his ear, wants him to know that he is safe. That he will never let Harrison go in this place of wave and mud. Below in the water, Bigfoot can feel a leech slide up his thigh and latch onto his scrotum. He pulls Harrison closer as the leech becomes a part of him so that, in the moonlight at Morgan Pond, it's impossible to tell them apart, Bigfoot and Harrison and leech, three in one, each drinking this moment, swelling into a fat black knot of love.

Bigfoot Remembers His Mother

Embrace of dung as he dug his face in her hairy breasts, nuzzled the mushrooms of her nipples, drank and drank as she moaned lullabies to the cups of his ears.

Squirrel and rabbit on her breath, the sweet copper of berry and bark. To this day, he cannot pass a raspberry bush or desiccated carcass without thinking of the cemetery of her teeth.

Trout and perch and salmon. How she lovingly tore open their silver bellies with her fingers, scooped guts into his mouth as the fish batted and gilled the air.

Hot August afternoons, she would carry him to the swamp, press him into the stagnant mud until his skin cooled and his back was a carpet of delicious mosquito.

She threw rocks big as raccoons at him, laughed her coyote laugh as they glanced off his head and the forest became a dizzy swarm of Ursids.

One day, he put his fist in a hornet's nest, felt the creatures inside boil up his hand and arm and shoulder. She spent three days sucking his fingers until they were soft as newborn mice.

He woke one night, and she was gone. For a week, he searched for her behind trees, in caves, ravines, on mountainsides. He found only a pile of empty oyster shells.

Tonight, he worries a radish-shaped scar on his brow, left by one of his mother's rocks. It reminds him of her thick toes.

Gaudete

He slouches through this night,
an eclipse of hair and muscle and foot,
guided by some wild nova
in the chambers of his Neanderthal
chest. It's an ancient story,
Precambrian even, about ice,
juniper berry in the deadest of winter.
Digging through dermal frost
to root and worm. Mushroom
caps in frozen moss, strips
of pine gnawed into sweet paste.
And moon held in knuckles of sumac.

Yes, it's about need and hunger,
a bottomless lake carved by glacier.
It's wilderness, the blind
sound of nebulae exploding seventy
million miles a day. Ice Age. Meteor
rain. Seraphim screaming hosannas
over panicked rams. Starlight and manure.
The coming of something
ferocious, untamable.

He knows all this somehow,
the way he knows where salmon leap, spawn.
He stands at the edge of a clearing,
stares up, into the hills, toward
an empty cave. He tilts back
his head, opens his throat, sings a song
for the evolution of love.

Bigfoot and Nessie: A Love Story

This is a meditation on flippers, the beauty of them. How they slice water like scaled swords, current moving hard and fast, as if on its way to some ancient Niagara scooped out by planes of ice.

This is also a meditation on feet. Toes as wide as canyons, heels that sink into the mud like meteors hurled from the sky to crush the world.

This is a meditation on neck, long and ribbed against a bowl of stars, a Triassic phalange playing the air like Mozart's ring finger, bending, dipping, disappearing, reappearing.

This is also a meditation on hairy shoulders big enough to push landslides back up mountains, hold in check mass extinction, stop evolution in its tracks with one soft grunt.

Above all, this is a meditation on attraction, how two large bodies are pulled toward each other despite their polarities. Negative calling to positive. Water calling to dirt. Cold-blooded to warm. Jurassic to Pliocene. Perhaps it will end in apocalypse, when these two bodies collide, atoms pinballing off each other in wild fusion, before they split apart, leaving behind Devonian ash and ruin.

Or maybe it will end at the bottom of a loch, buried under wave and peat and clay. An egg, holding an embryo, furred, scaled. Something new to reset the alarm clock of the universe.

Bigfoot Has Late Fees
at the Carnegie Library

I let go, over and over, every day.
Let go of sleep when sun
forces stars to let go of sky.
Let go of hunger when bacon
snaps like knuckles in the pan.
Let my daughter go in the Malibu
with the boy who looks at her
as if tomorrow the world will end
and she holds the key to the fallout
shelter somewhere in her body.
Watch my mother let go, drift
back to sometime before
she met my father when she was still
the center of gravity, everything
revolving around the jitterbug
of her hips. Whisper to my father,
tell him it's okay to let go,
wave his white flag, climb
out of his foxhole, cross the field
into the enemy's arms.

Bigfoot doesn't understand
this need in his cave somewhere
in the hills, filled with sweet
pine boughs, wild raspberry,
venison and salt. As frost
curls the maple leaves outside,
he rereads some borrowed
pages in the dark with his
nocturnal eyes. Maybe the one
about the old man and the marlin.
Goes back to the beginning,
before the sharks come,
when the fish is whole,
big as a Cadillac, pulling

the old man's boat out and out
toward that place where the earth
curves, bends, lets go, where ancient
sailors fell off the edge of the planet,
into the throats of sea monsters.

**White-tailed deer and Lady Bigfoot
on the Banks of Au Sable River,
Lake Superior Region, Michigan,
1903. Photograph by George Shiras**

She is night,
just above the young buck's
velvet prongs, her firefly
eyes hovering in jacklight;
the deer doesn't care
about the camera's mushroom
flash blowing over the slap of sable
water, worries more about
what he cannot see—
black hole of breast, leg, arm,
fishy maw caught the second
before, when the deer's spine,
haunches, and neck coil,
when everything wide angles,
the world etched
in isinglass, waiting, waiting
for the savage descent—but not now,
not in this heartbeat near
a midnight tongue of river, framed
by log, reed, limb, shoreline,
crickets silenced mid-shrill,
waves frozen mid-purl,
like the photo of a breath
held above a cake, candles
guttering
for eternity.

Lady Bigfoot Kept Him in Her Cave

Few know Love so large it eclipses bird and brook, wind and forest, reef and ocean. For most, it's the flash of deer tail in woods, rabbit shadow in moss and moon. That small, that fast, that fleeting. It's the silver tongue of frost on grass, hungry for sun. And when sun comes, there is an instant of abandon, chimerical, ice and light and mist at once. A beat, a blink, then a field of green tears.

The Love he knows has granite arms and bear breath that swallows you like blueberries, big, round, and sweet. See it, tall and wide as redwoods. Hear it, a wild howl, half-human, half-wolf. A universe of limb and muscle, the fierce gravity of lip, shoulder, and breast. Ravenous.

Every day, it takes hold, leads him through the cave, through blackness so black he loses skin, that atlas of form and touch, of ecstasy. Surrender is an ant and grub. Fern and apple. Cloud and rain. All of it.

Bigfoot Takes His Wife to Mount Rushmore for Their Honeymoon

Roosevelt watches as they come together on Lincoln's hair, become an avalanche of finger, tongue, arm, leg. They make buffalo noises, passenger pigeon noises that haven't been heard since before McKinley became extinct in New York. Under Roosevelt's granite gaze, the Bigfoots do what they have been doing for hundreds of years, when Washington's teeth were still in the mouths of slaves, when the quills Jefferson wrote "We hold these truths" were still helping ducks and geese wing south.

They bite neck, shoulder, paw and plow fields of thigh, let high "Star Spangled Banner" sounds spill under the milkweed stars. Wild for fur, skin, they earthquake into each other, unite their states without Constitution or Congress. No walls or borders stop them. Their guiding torch, the tug and pull of tempest-tost heart. They are spacious sky, amber wave, beautiful pilgrim feet.

And below them, the stone faces stare into the distance, the way bachelor uncles and maiden aunts do at weddings, embarrassed by the sway and grind of that first slow dance.

A Bruise the Shape of Bigfoot

sits on my thigh, arm stretched toward my groin,
as if supporting what sits in the fork of my legs.
How did this raspberry beast lumber across my skin?
I remember no collision with door, no stumble
in midnight dark. It was simply there one day,
full blown, has remained for several weeks,
as if afraid to move on. Perhaps it is frightened,
doesn't want to escape, the hematoma of its body
tattooed in place. Or maybe it's simply content,
has found a warm place to stay without worry of hunter,
hunger. I say goodnight, cover it with pajama,
tuck it in, the way I do with my son, saying
a prayer, wishing it safety and love
in the cave of my flesh.

Bigfoot Goes Trick-or-Treating

It's time to come out of the trees,
lumber through wookies and Dark Knights,
step over Little Mermaids, Maleficents,
bump into sexy nurses, high-five zombies.
A night to collect prizes for being
big as a Clydesdale, for having feet
that carve valleys in sidewalks.

First prize, a popcorn ball for weighing
as much as Lincoln's Rushmore nose.
Snickers for having arms that reach
across January to frogs singing
Handel's *Messiah* in June swamps.
And Twix, his favorite, for being something
he can't help: a throwback.
Genetic link or mishap. Extra
chromosome, hyperactive gland.
Bearded lady. Alligator boy.
Lon Chaney, wolf drunk on moonlight.
He goes door-to-door, holds out
a palm the size of an earthquake,
collects sweetness that he counts
as proof of the existence of love.
He spends the rest of his year
chasing it through streams, up
sides of mountains, into blizzards.

Bigfoot Multiple Choice Haibun

after W. Todd Kaneko

Bigfoot growled last night in my backyard where banks hunched like marble surf, a cemetery of ice. My dog, fur a mini-map of the world, squatted in a yoga pose of defecation. I stood, stared into midnight's mouth, heard it. Low as the separation of sea and shore, crabapple and crawfish. A haired wall of mud and sand and God's toes rolled over us both. My dog sniffed, raised her muzzle, buried her nose in constellations, made the sound of pharaohs being sealed in their pyramids, a wail that opened the gates of Duat. And I knew I was about to become a footprint, a skunk-filled memory.

Question: What do you do when Bigfoot growls?

    a) Let your dog eat a meteor.
    b) Sink into earth like salt.
    c) Become an eardrum.

Bigfoot's New Year's Resolutions

he wants to gain weight
stand in the middle of woods
be mistaken for a landslide

he wants to exercise less
find a pine stump, sit on it
until his muscles turn to clay

he wants to eat more meat
every day find something furred, young
gnash, rip, floss his teeth with its skin

he wants to drink more
fill a creek bed with apples
swim and gulp the sweet rot

he wants more clutter
an old couch from the dump
newspapers that smell like perch

he wants to care less
piss in the mouth of the Chocolay
shit on the beach, not bury it

he wants to travel less
remain in his cedared cave
read long chapters of winter, sleep

he wants less time with his wife
let her take their young and leave
spend days gobbling silence like honey

he wants to procrastinate more
wake in afternoon sun, not hunt
until owls dissect the moon

Bigfoot Yoga

Hold *Sukhasana*,
in green lungs of forest
from now until rapture, when the hairy
back of time splits open
like a mustard kernel, spreads,
stretches into footprints so yellow
they put the sun to shame as it troops
across July.

Hold this pose until who you are
can only be found in museum
diorama crowded with dodos. This
is where ohms quake over you,
the way passenger pigeons shattered
day with the slap of their wings.
Be brave. Open your mouth. Find
that place where walls sweat
with shaman, mammoth hunt.
Allow yourself to hunch, ape over,
devolve downward,
downward until you are
what we once were:
Bone. Clay.
Breath
of Bigfoot.

Slow Dancing with Bigfoot
in Greenwich

This has been Bigfoot's stool
even before he handed Marsha P.
that brick when the Betty Badges
pounded on the door, shouted,
"Police! We're taking the place!"
the same night Judy G. was buried.
Now, he nurses sloe gins,
listens to piped-in "Over the Rainbow,"
homage to friends left behind.

Vinnie the Cheek, black-haired and beautiful,
used to call him "honey," scratched
his shoulders with cattail fingers.
Angel from the Bronx, in fishnets, heels,
baked him brownies, told him over and over
how the carpet of his arms reminded Angel
of his grandfather in Puerto Rico.
Montana Bill, quiet as a cow, sat beside
Bigfoot, inhaled his fishy cologne,
ate pretzels, cried about the way
his dad's denim jacket smelled
like horse and coffee in the mornings.
So many more. So many. Lost
in the Reagan years. Now just forgotten
patches on an immense quilt.

Bigfoot is at home here. Nobody stares
at the taxi of his back, piles of peanut
shells in his beard, on the mountain
of his belly. He doesn't have to hide
in the bathroom, stare through windows,
on the limen between evolution and myth.
He sits at the bar, among reflections
in mirror, in bottles, dozens of Bigfoots
spinning, swimming, shimmering.

Every once in a while, someone asks
him to dance. Walks him to the dim
floor, rests a head against his leathery breast.
Sways to George Michael, Etta James,
"Careless Whisper" or "At Last." Slow.
Always slow songs. *Ignorance is kind.*
There's no comfort in the truth.
After the music ends, his partner will lean
in, press lips to his cheek, thank him
for the dance, for being King of the Forest,
arm-in-arm with Dorothy,
skipping toward the Emerald City.

a bigfoot bestiary and other wonders

Pablo Auditions Bigfoot
to Replace the Minotaur

He is triangle stacked on triangle,
    head triangle balanced on shoulder
    triangle tapered to leg triangle.
Obtuse and acute, right and scalene,
    hypotenuse as long as the equator,
    devoid of curve or horizon or sunset.
His eyes, tiny, yellow equilaterals
    beneath a brow that defies
    Pythagoras.
Mouth, teeth, a Stonehenge
    of angles placed just so
    to capture the orange secants of solstice.
He is fractal,
    a mirror of big and small,
    Bigfoot within Bigfoot within Bigfoot.
He doesn't fit Blue,
    Rose or African, barely squeezes his
    isoscelean bulk beside *The King of the Minotaurs*.
Stretched across canvas,
    a study of concentric,
    tangent, clusters of Venn.
He remains unfinished,
    abandoned,
because a frame cannot contain so big a heart.

Frost and Bigfoot Duet in the Great Dismal Swamp

after Robert Frost's "The Most of It"

Young Frost bellowed his moosey
yawp, chin tilted toward the vertebrae
of cypresses pressing black sky.
He expected nothing. No cool finger
tracing his fevered neck,
no lavender skin or corn silk
hair. He was alone
with mosquitoes big as bricks,
water moccasins gliding through chocolate
pools, the hungry slurp of moss and mud.
Surrendered all his verses
to this one prehistoric bawl. A cave sound.
The gnaw of a wounded mammoth heart.

Thigh-deep in bog, Bigfoot knew
the Neanderthal ballad Frost was singing,
had heard it before he crawled out
from between his mother's redwood
thighs. It was the song of the universe
during the great cleaving, when gas and light
screamed on the front porch, divorced
forever. Bigfoot carried all of that
on the apocalypse of his shoulders,
each mass extinction, ice age,
each dodo, passenger pigeon,
each evolution of the broken heart.
He raised his lips to the trees,
roared back at Frost, a Big Bang
of loss that expanded and contracted
the swamp to its foundations.

Frost leaped on the road, his skin's
cells rearranged by grief's
refrain. Before Einstein
scribbled relativity down on a used napkin,

the poet felt fission dwarf him,
envisioned an elk emerging
from the crumpled water
of a lake, shaking it off in a great
watery veil. Frost raised his chin,
bellowed again into the black divide.

Bigfoot and Charlie Parker—Mardi Gras, 1950

Bigfoot had a thing for jazz
ever since he heard Bird
in the cedar swamp, horn
stuttering in moss and marsh
like a timber wolf with hiccups,
a moose and rhino in rut, clouds
of hungry flies on a July beach.
He followed that sound, found
Bird sitting on a stump,
fingers moving so fast and hard
on that gold stick that Bigfoot
thought he was killing it
for dinner, wringing every
last drop of life out of its ribs,
making it scream so beautifully
that constellations stopped dead
in their tracks to listen. Bird nodded
at him, kept playing,
up through laced branches,
down into mud and root,
crying, howling, bansheeing
until even the cypresses
snapped their reed fingers.
Then Bird paused, looked at him,
said, "You're one big bastard, man,"
stood up, started blowing again,
strutting, swinging his sax,
and Bigfoot followed, clapping,
stomping, waving his arms, not
caring who saw his missing link
ass parading all the way down
to Bourbon Street, snatching beads
out of the air like Jesus collecting
souls on Judgment Day.

A Good Hominid Is Hard to Find

Flannery wasn't into beauty:
dolls and doilies and needlepoint.
Gravity pulled her to bantams
that strutted backwards. Carnivals
where intersexed people spouted
Gospel. Eucharist suns that bled
across Georgia dusk. And Bigfoot.
She loved him as if her salvation
depended on it. When she couldn't
walk any more, he carried her
around Andalusia, so she could
hear stupid cows bellow, see
peafowl blossom into resurrection.
When she sat at her Remington,
he stood outside her bedroom window,
listened to her machine gun fingers
as they chased misfits moving
through pine branches like noon
grace. She thought Bigfoot
was a hairy Pentecost in her feeble
life. In the hospital, when she died,
perhaps she saw him enter her room,
scoop her up, cradle her against
his thick breast, carry her
down a highway where
cicada sawed the heavens in two.

Perkins and Bigfoot Skip Stones at Eagle Pond

for Donald Hall

Perkins likes to talk.
Bigfoot likes to listen.
They both like the gush
of mud between their toes,
water slurping their ankles.
Perkins says sunlight
in the pond pierces his old eyes
like barbed wire. Bigfoot licks
an ant off Perkins's forehead.
Perkins says June days
cuckoo by, sunup to sundown,
each second a stone skipped
across the surface until
it sinks. Bigfoot spits
in Perkins's hair,
parts and smooths its thicket.
Perkins says he's tired
of how each grass
blade and greening leaf touches
him with his wife's buried
fingertips. Bigfoot stands silent
beside him. Unwritten.

Bigfoot Meets a Homeless Man on Presque Isle

The man smells wild,
the way a black bear smells
after winter sleep, full
of hunger, root, and dark. Bigfoot
can taste loneliness on the man,
a sweaty slick of days spent near
the big water, hidden in pine,
rooting through garbage cans
for leftover French fries, brown
apple cores still sweet and seeded,
hot dog buns gone chlorophyll green.
                    Bigfoot knows
this man will die soon,
has seen it before when moose
with brain worm stumble off
by themselves, or one eaglet shreds
a feebler eaglet to get
more perch and salmon from
their mother's beak. Even this close
to lights and cars and houses, survival
is all about being bigger, stronger,
hairier, scaling trees for nested
eggs, scooping spottails from Superior
surf, tearing haunches off mewling fawns.
                    Bigfoot wants
to help the man who has wandered
onto this rocky thumb surrounded by wave.
Hopes he feels as wanted
as soft leaves or a run of smelt.
As the man beds down for the night
under a ribcage of branches, Bigfoot
knuckles one tree trunk, knocks, knuckles
again, knocks. He does this until
he hears hollow, then scratch, chatter.
He plunges his hand into the tree,

extracts a panicked squirrel. Bigfoot snaps
its neck like a cricket leg. Holds
the carcass to his chest, breathes the last
pulses of its pebble heart, then grunts
a prayer of thanks.
               Bigfoot leaves
the squirrel at the man's sleeping
feet, where he'll find it in morning
light. An offering of meat, blood, fur.
To remind the man that the world
still loves him.

Bigfoot Tries to Fix
His Daughter's Broken Heart

Since he only knows how to pray with fingers thick as squirrels, he fills her cave with spider webs, traps her sobs, cocoons them, and,

since the ground is still too frozen to dig a grave, takes them down to the lake to drown.

Since he wants to remind her she's alive, he takes her to the valley where she was born, where he first baptized her frog body in great, salty gulps.

Since he doesn't know the word "love," he paints her face with clay. Tenderly, with his tongue.

Since heartbreak isn't a porcupine he can crush with a rock.

Since she feels abandoned, he gives her ribs of a deer bleached by sun. To hug herself. They splinter after one day, become dander and crumb.

Since she feels unimportant, he brings a skunk to her, places it on her head like a crown.

Since love doesn't blossom like mushrooms in mud and rot, moves faster than flea or shadow.

Since she won't eat, he collects fistfuls of spring peepers, scoops them between her lips. They sing in her mouth.

Bigfoot Visits a Sick Friend

for Daniel

Daniel is all tornado—unable
to find shelter in this muscle
storm. His face swings north,
shoulders heave west, fingers drum
the table like fat bullets of rain.
He's been trying to drink the same
milk carton for an hour, lowers
his lips to straw before another
cyclone spasms them away,
carries him south then
east again. He lifts a spoon
of apple sauce, aims
it at his mouth, thrusts it
forward. Convulsions drive
his hand northwest, sauce landing
somewhere near his ear.
He begins the process again. Milk. Straw.
Spoon. Apple sauce. Keeps trying to steer
his body to safe harbor.

Bigfoot watches this struggle,
stands in a corner, silent. He doesn't
understand these warm and cold fronts
battling across Daniel's body. He
reaches out, hugs his friend, breathes
deep forest over him. His friend
hurricanes, blizzards, earthquakes
against his chest. He holds Daniel,
glides glacier fingers across his friend's
forehead, through his hair. Lets
ice age landlock them both until the room
fills with planes and planes of white.

Bigfoot is a land bridge from Russia to Alaska
that mammoth herds crossed in search

     a bigfoot bestiary and other wonders

of things green and warm. He cups
Daniel's hand, guides
him over the tundra
to a place
where ripe
blueberries
grow.

Bigfoot Gets Mistaken for John the Baptist
at the Church of Corpus Christi

Perhaps it's the smell of dead
grasshoppers, wild honey
in his beard. Maybe the heaving
camel humps of his shoulders,
dirt crusted under his toenails,
in creases of his soles.
It may be his eyes, that
forty-day-in-the-desert-without-food
famish, how he watches the priest's
fingers raise a white moon,
up and up.

Bigfoot huffs
the air, fills his nostril caves
with the promise of flesh and blood.
He stands, moves into the aisle,
strides as wide as the Jordan,
and the faithful fall back, watch
with interest his hirsute
advance. Bigfoot towers over
the priest, eyes the thin wafer of light.
He tilts his head to the vaulted ceiling,
opens his mouth, makes a noise, splits
the heavens in two, and the flock
beholds what a voice crying out
in the wilderness sounds like.

Bigfoot Celebrates
His 251st Birthday

Rubs his feet against
the spines of a dead porcupine,
enjoys how the barbs lance
a deep itch in his soles
that has plagued him
since he turned 201 and found
he couldn't bend over anymore
to touch his boulder toes.

Gnaws the ribs of a moose,
cracks them open, slurps
the soup inside, even though
his gut will earthquake for days.

Stares at his wife's hairy backside,
remembers when he was 187,
and they would shake the forest
with love ten or 12 times a day
until it was wrung empty
of doe and grizzly and boar.

Sucks the rock his mother
threw at him when he was 12,
broke his nose, how she licked
blood off his face, laughed
like a morning crow, and he'd kept it,
worried it ever since until it was
soft, smooth as an eyelid.

Waits to hear his son or daughter
whoop in the green air, to let him
know they haven't forgotten him,
may bring the young by later
so he can tell them the story
of how he once wrestled a snake

from the heavens, its back shooting
with milk and star and comet shine,
tied that snake into a fist, pitched
that fist back into the dark sky
where it still rolls, sundown to up,
fills the pines with light.

FURRED AND WINGED AND SCALED

"So God created great sea creatures and every living thing that moves ..."
    —Genesis 1:12 NKJV

"Any glimpse into the life of an animal quickens our own and makes it so much larger and better in every way."
    —John Muir

Doe After a Blizzard

My son noticed her first, splayed, bloody, broken by a neighbor's fence.

A dead doe, shining in the sunlight that always comes after a blizzard,

sunlight so strong it hurts to step into it. Sunlight that shouts.

The doe was haloed in that light, and my son, only five, said,

Fix it, Daddy, reduced me to an Easter Island moai, stone face

immutable in the presence of suffering. I wanted to tell my son

I can't or *She's gone* or *She's with God* or some other

emptiness recited in church every Sunday so often that it has lost

its ability to comfort. Instead, I picked my son up, carried him

closer to the doe, whispered in his ear *Isn't she beautiful?*

I watched his face change, confusion give way to something

seraphic. *Yes*, he said, nodding. *Yes, she is. Yes. Yes. Yes. Yes.*

A Pig's Orgasm Lasts 30 Minutes

This from a pig farmer who hasn't slept in two weeks.

His wife left him. His children, one by one, have disappeared, leaving notes on the kitchen table: "I am tired of so much passion."

Now that he is alone, some nights, the pig farmer stumbles into the barn to watch the swine orgy, listen to their sweaty foreplay, satisfied thrusting grunts. And then, after several minutes, the moment arrives. Long and loud as an air raid siren, it goes on and on and on and on. The cows in their stalls look up with envy, the mares in the corral nicker, tremble in want.

And the pig farmer sits in the manure pile, wonders if his wife still wears her wedding ring.

Call of the Yellow Dog Wild Woman

for Judith Minty

I saw her
a long time ago,
when fingers of cedar
cupped
a Eucharist moon,
when the Yellow Dog
bloomed
with winter melt.
Her hair
jeweled
with birch leaves
jived
around her face
like field mice
hungry
in a crib of corn.
Her will-o'-the-wisp
breasts and legs
knit
and purled
white fire
through hemlocks,
her skunky scent
hugging
the air with thick
Bigfoot arms.
And when she
aimed
her chin upward,
opened
the braids
of her lips,
her wild song
brimmed
the mug of night,

begged
Ursa
to lumber,
charge,
invade
her pine
den where she
would welcome
him, let him
rest
his starry muzzle
on her thigh,
stroke
his rough back,
pull
him closer,
love
him
'til dawn.

Blueberrying

I can feel the muscles of my calves, thighs
tight as birch bark, cramped from being
bear, nosing along the ground in search
of sweet bits of sky tethered to ground
by stem. They cluster there in cough
and hiss, the waves of Superior eating
beach behind my hunched back.
I scoop with my paws, strip
with my teeth. They fill my mouth
with all that is tender and sweet
in the mosquito heat
of August.

Chipmunks See in Slow Motion

We are Charlie Chaplins to them, shamble across streets, canes swinging in orbits at our sides. Each breath, convulse of heart—a Grand Canyon that chipmunks stand on the lip of, gaze into with the kind of wonder we reserve for births, deaths, healing the blind.

Think of that *City Lights* moment, Virginia Cherrill, her vision newborn in a world of daffodil, baby's breath, gazes into Chaplin's convict eyes, knows in slow motion palm caress, pinkie glide that love is a cigar stub smoking in the gutter. And the bud of Chaplin's face starts to blossom, unfold. Petal gives way to petal gives way to pistil gives way to stamen until eventually we are staring at a Georgia O'Keeffe canvas, a flowered landscape of joyous hunger.

No wonder chipmunks hibernate all winter. What creatures can exist in such an overcranked world of summer burgeon and not need to prick a finger on a spinning wheel, nap until love's true fingertips rescue them from 120 frames-per-second oblivion?

Portrait of the Virgin Mary as Skunk

She shambles, slow as a mud puddle,
bright arm of lightning splitting
the night of her body, peacock
plume tail sweeping the ground
behind her, the way, I imagine,
Mary swept sawdust from her floors
after Joseph was done for the day.

And think of that smell, part terror,
part warning. Mary calling
her son to supper, him ignoring her,
turning stones into toads, leaves
into salamanders. When he didn't
answer, Mary unleashed her quiet
wrath until it settled on his godly
skin, pickled him in maternal love.

Whitman and the Skunk

I see you on the shore of Superior, water
curling around your blue feet. In your arms,
a skunk pressed into the capacious swirls
of your gray beard, cradled like a wounded
soldier. This creature, black hole body
shot with nova light, trusts you,
knows that you contain cannon
fire and lilac, armies of geese in winter
retreat, salmon sun leaping into
dawn, yawn of dusk in oak
bough. Shin deep in this arctic sea,
the smell of you mixes with
the smell of him. God, you're both
so beautiful and electric
in your love!

Stealing a Last Line from Keith Taylor

Morning darkness, I stand
ankle-deep in snow. My dog
noses through cold and white
while I stare at a moon
veiled in winter cloud.

The world shrinks, expands
at once, as if we are
the only two living beings
left—my dog and me.
As if we stand just before
the fatal comet crashes down
or after the universe contracts

into a tight fist that will blossom
into creation. I know
here, at the cusp of dawn,
everything will soon start
to stretch and yawn.

I see a flash of movement.
A rabbit sprints to a berm
of hibernating lilacs, disappears
into the earth, to its warren
of waiting, hungry kits.

I cannot believe our world is dying.

Night Canticle and Other Loose Change

In the middle of sleepless night, couch my space

while moon, constellations creep by outside

like hungry skunks. Even sound has gone to bed,

and what I'm left with is nothing.

But you. Faithful friend, who didn't want

crate or pillow, treat or knot. You sit with your muzzle

on my thigh, gray back studded with continents of black.

I rest my hand on you, press fingers into the tiny

atlas of your shoulders, and you huff out

a sigh as long as summer. I feel its El Nino

warmth on my skin. Now I understand why

Saint Francis preached to sparrow flocks

and hungry wolves. They accept this world

for just what it is: an aggie rattling around

with loose pennies and nickels

in God's deep, wide pocket.

One Dog

after Richard Blanco's "One Today"

Yes, this is one of those dog poems
full of leather tongue, wet noses pressed
into crotches. Because dogs are all about
hope. For backyard hunts of gray
squirrels or screeching jays.
For a piece of hotdog bun to flake off,
fall to hardwood floor. A fly
in the water dish, flash of mouse
in corner dark. A dog survives
on hope, from first yawn and stretch
to pillow sigh.

Hope is also what wags
the leash, digs in a box for a bone-
shaped biscuit. At night, hope
slams the car door, enters the house,
calls out, sings out *Good girl!* or *Good boy!*
Which is an invocation, a conjuring.

Yes, hope is a four-legged thing
that meets you after a long day
of reports and budgets, shivers its tail,
helicopters on the floor, humps
your shins, circles and circles and circles
until, exhausted, it flops on its back,
waits for your hand to reach down,
scratch its belly until it pisses
all over you in joy.

Butterflies Taste with Their Feet

nibble the world with each step, flit like debutantes from one cotillion to another. They don't glut or gorge. They're dainty in their waltzes, summer dresses.

I loved a butterfly once, took her to movies where she nestled on my buttery fingers as I ate popcorn. Brought her home for Thanksgiving. My mother smiled, said she had a good appetite, landing on the white meat, dark meat, canned cranberry, Stove Top stuffing, pumpkin pie.

Ours was a romance for the ages. Romeo and Juliet. Jane Eyre and Rochester. Shakespeare and his Dark Lady. Me and my butterfly, her wings the color of carrot and saffron. She would crawl over my body, taste my skin. I still dream of our time together.

At rosy-fingered dawn, I find myself blossoming, bursting open, unfolding my petals toward the long light of day. My pillow still smells of pollen.

A Duck's Quack Doesn't Echo

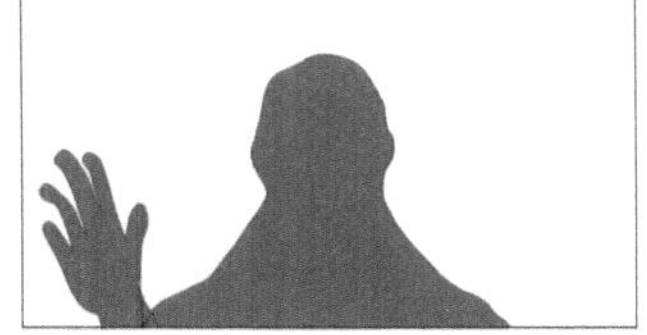

scalpels through everything. Cloud. Pine. Mountain. Redwood. Ocean. A duck quacked over the Grand Canyon. Six days later, a woman named Chunua heard that quack in the midnight sky of Wuhan.

Named by her mother, because, on the day she was born, years before the coughing started, cherry blossoms filled the lungs of the trees with sweetness and beauty. *You are Chunua*, her mother said, *my spring flower*. And she flourished in the hothouse of her mother's arms.

When Chunua heard that quack last night, she thought it was her mother's ghost in the bare cherry trees. Still fevered. Breath hard as an apricot pit. Chunua stopped. Listened. Not wanting to let her go again. Pressed a ghost hand to her face, felt her mother's love dancing like bees against the petals of her lips.

An Elephant Leap of Faith

Elephants are the only animals that cannot jump, perhaps for the same reason they cannot fly: the weight of bone. They lumber place to place, heads down, think of all things they cannot do. They cannot play leapfrog, celebrate leap year. Despise the TV show *Quantum Leap* and Little Orphan Annie with her "leapin' lizards!" Envy salmon their upstream leaps. Have never looked before they leapt, or leapt to a conclusion.

When Armstrong took his one small step, one giant leap, they made their way to a graveyard, stood among ribs of grandparents, aunts, uncles, raised their trunks to the tusk of moon, bellowed against the gravity of their existence, forever bound by toe and foot to mud, clay, clods of dirt.

At night, in their grief, they shudder. Snore. Dream of feathers, ibis, kingfisher. Feel a divine nudge to take one, deep elephantine breath, start to walk. Then lope. Gallop. Charge. Ears scooping, tails ruddering. Faster. Faster. Faster. Until—

It happens. Wind takes over, and they lift, rise, keep rising, great gray kites. They swoop, dip, circle. Up and up, to Aegean blue and light and sun. Like an exaltation of larks winging south, they grow small, smaller, smallest, vanish into a parade of ivory clouds.

Bodies of Water

We're all bodies of water,
contain within our shores
tides, waves, bends in rivers,
trout sinking to silt bed,
loons weeping over cattail marsh.
That's why, in the drought of night,
my son calls for water, gulps it
down like a thirsty black bear
when I bring it to him. He must
still remember when breath
flowed through his gills
in that blue hydrosphere
of beginning.

Naming Things in Big Sur

A bird perches on the railing.
If I was in Michigan, it would
be a blue jay. Since I am
in California, it could be
anything—a blue brushed throttle
or a cerulean sea sparrow.
I am in a new place, unfamiliar
with the names of things.

This green stuff under my toes,
I will know it as emerald kiss.
This small orange flower
shall be christened tiger tin.
Growing outside my cabin door,
purple widow's heart, tall,
straight as a broom handle.
The five-petaled red blossoms
down by the waterfalls,
shall be Bethlehem moss.
Spilling down the cliff face,
lemming bushes and holy spirits
with their snowy bowls, gold eyes.
At dusk, they glow
like white hummingbirds.
In the tree behind me,
a bird I can't see
coughs and hence
shall be known
as a tuberculin trill.

I know this place now,
can rest here under
the Bigfoot banyans.
I will lay my head on the stump
of this Magdalene magpie and sleep,
listen to the waves of the big blue

inhaling and exhaling the shore.
I shall call it Beth's Breath.

Ode to Kurt's Ashes in McLane Creek

Ghosts come to this green place
where bush and tree and water meet.
They stand, let the creek flow
over and through their fleshless
toes, listen to the burp and chuck
as mud gathers, twigs glide toward
Puget Sound and Olympia and Seattle.
Jim and Amy sit zazen on the banks,
let ants, crickets pass through
them like parings of rock
flinting through midnight,
striking comets in their spectral bodies.
Janis and Jimi raise their arms,
dance a slow bump and slide together
in a morning haze of purple
that hugs the ground close, waits
for injections of sun to fill the day's
veins with birdlight and birdsong.
Kurt has been here before and before,
his atoms soaked in the loamy
discharge, chanted through this bardo
by deer tongue, gulped by black
bear, Bigfoot, gritted by clam into
something beautiful: a pearled spirit,
polished with the smell of becoming.

Catfish Have 27,000 Taste Buds

but spend their lives at rock bottom of river, crick, marsh, with no ambition to rise. They comb their whiskers with clay, savor each intimate piece of universe that enters their bodies.

They are algae, crawfish, caddis fly, frog, clam, blueberry. Munch up and down the food chain, frequent greasy spoons and Michelin stars. A catfish once ate an eagle feather, dreamed of clouds, sky for weeks. Another swallowed a used condom, felt guilty for cheating on his wife.

Cut a catfish open, you might find car keys you lost last Friday, or your sister who died of lymphoma five years ago. Dinosaurs or ice ages, dark matter or da Vinci. One catfish contains multitudes, feeds 5,000, with 15 baskets left over for breakfast.

Nietzsche said God is dead. He isn't. He's inside a catfish belly, playing pinochle, waiting to be caught, filleted, breaded, fried into rapture with grits.

Ode to Tapioca

for Gideon

Just off the stove,
it sweats
after playing tag
with the whisk
in August boil.
At night,
it calms, sleeps,
burps vanilla.
Few people care
for its curd warmth,
how it rolls
on the tongue
like frog eggs,
stuff used to bait
hooks, catch
rainbow trout,
its name
a swamp sound,
galumph of hairy feet
through quag and sump.
In morning sun,
it sits politely
on my spoon,
and I say to it,
"Not everyone
will like you
today. That's okay."

Koi

for A. C.

They blossom in ripples, Monet
creatures, fuzzy at the edges, suffused
with a kind of radioactive light.
The old Japanese man created
this pond, perhaps from some haiku
by Basho. *Here, in the lake. Fish float.*
God's eyelashes flash. Perhaps
from a recollection of Kyoto
where his father suckled the umbra
of his grandmother's young breasts.
Or perhaps he just woke up
one morning, aching
for something beautiful, went
to work. Van Gogh in an Arles
field. Michelangelo on a slab
of David marble. Him hauling
a copper bucket of kumquat
fish that orbited the starry
water, the way my pen
chases this poem's end
like Halley's Comet
through hungry,
white space
toward the gravity
of its last breath.

One Species of Jellyfish Is Immortal

moves from polyp to medusa to polyp over and over. Which came first—jellyfish or God? Book of Jellyfish, Chapter 1, Verse 1: *In the beginning was jellyfish, and jellyfish was with God, and jellyfish was God.*

Before the first day, light and dark, before God even breathed, there was jellyfish in a blue nirvana of brine and tears. Which means that before there was heart, there was heartbreak. Jellyfish and God fractals. Grief within grief within grief.

If you get stung by jellyfish or God, don't urinate on yourself to cleanse the poison. That's a tale told by old sailors who chase St. Elmo's votives. If you are touched by God/tendril of jellyfish, you are a chosen one. Bearer of a sadness that has existed before existence. Wail, gnash, hosanna your teeth. Something is about to be born again. Its natal starfish blazes in coral skies. Follow it to tide pools. Sargasso kelp. Stop. Listen.

You will hear your daughter's first breath move over the waters, beginning calling to beginning.

Starfish Have No Brains

so they can't assemble pieces to create a whole picture.

They live on image and instant. Emerald sea. First kiss. Coral. Parrot fish and salt. Long embraces, arm in arm in arm in arm in arm. Moonlit beach, tide. Bark of seal. Coming together. Seagull shriek. Collision of heavenly bodies. Crab scuttle. Separation. Moan of whale under black skies. Emptiness.

If the starfish had a brain, he would throw himself into barracuda jaw, cormorant beak. Allow himself to bake in sun.

Instead, he just counts waves. One wave. One wave. One wave. One wave. Never getting to two.

Spring Choirs

Spring crickets and peepers were loud as interstate traffic tonight, calling and singing to each other under gauzed light. I turned off the living room lamp, shut the windows, put my lunch in the fridge for tomorrow, then went out my front door, stood barefoot in the grass, listened to the choirs of insect and amphibian, with an occasional dog tenor or baritone. That instant the universe seemed all right, as if nothing could be wrong anywhere in its vast concert hall. No discord of plague or war. No disharmonies of famine or hatred. Just wet grass and mud under my toes, dark fingers of lilac branches reaching up to the starry, starry keyboard of night. And the crickets and peepers serenading moon and comets and cosmic dust.

Try it now. Slow everything down to the life span of a cricket. Until one breath is a minute, hour, day, month, year, decade, century, generation, era, epoch. Until that breath spills out like a woodwind in an orchestra, playing one, true, clear note into the ear of the universe.

The Ugliest Fish in North America

for Lydia

The mother worries about DNA, how helix
can twist, like shadows on bedroom walls,
into something terrifying, tree into banshee,
chair into dragon, son into a person
she'd avoid on street corners, thin
as a blade of grass, arms full of purple
canals, a universe of scabby stars.
She wonders how the collision of egg
with sperm inside her belly created
this creature so drawn to the smell
of carbon monoxide, the taste of razor.
From where in the evolution of family
did this vestigial finger or toe of insanity
come? Was it grandpa from Buffalo,
who got drunk at Niagara Falls, walked
the railing like a Wallenda, one arm
stretched toward his new bride,
the other toward thunder, mist, oblivion?
Was it great-grandma from Russia,
who buried two daughters in wheat
fields before they could suckle because
they were daughters, couldn't work the earth
from rock and frost into mud, into yam,
corn, cabbage? Or was it someone she
didn't know, someone further than memory,
who planted this seed in her tree,
this son flower who now fills her pillows
with the wail of loon over moon and lake?
One day when she was a girl, she stood
in the shallows of Superior, her body just
a promise of woman, mother. She felt
a monster slide by her in the water,
larger than her father, a freight, all
cartilage and fin, scute and armor,
a live fossil against her skin. She reached out,

touched its flank, her fingers connected
to a thing ancient: carnosaurus, tarbosaurus,
pteranodon. It moved slower than glacier,
gave her time to know its prehistoric form,
shape unchanged by seventy million years
of spawn and weed, the skim for minnow,
mayfly, mosquito. As a girl, the mother
didn't fear this car of a fish, instead accepted
its presence as blessing, Paraclete, spirit
to pass on to her mother, father, mate, child.
Beside her son's hospital bed today, she watches
him, counts his breaths, wants to press
her thumb to the flutter in his wrist.
She thinks of Longfellow's hero, swallowed
by the sturgeon, crawling down its throat,
through rib, toward the drumming darkness.
She closes her eyes, wraps her arms around
Nahma's great heart, lets it throb, convulse
against her face and breasts, hears blood
roaring in and out, to gill, brain, nose, tail.
She holds on the way she now wants to hold
her son. To save him, reverse Darwin, genetics.
Force him backwards to the time when his life
was still cretaceous, a mystery. A shining,
black egg in the vast water of her womb.

   a bigfoot bestiary and other wonders

CODA

"Then God saw everything that he had made, and indeed it was very good."
—Genesis 1:31 NKJV

"I must go in, for the fog is rising."
—The last words of Emily Dickinson

On Your 60th Birthday

for Sally

This birdsong morning, you have been free of rib and lung for almost seven years. You've seen the face of God or disappeared down oblivion's throat. Soared with seraphim or fed the veins of hungry cedars. Mystery doesn't exist where you are now, or you have become part of mystery. Remember the first question we learned in catechism? *Who made you?* Answer: *God made me.* Second question: *Who is God?* Second answer: *God is the supreme being who made all things.* We recited those words as simple as vanilla pudding, rolled them around on our tongues, swallowed them as easy as breath. Perhaps it is that plain. Perhaps, after your last sigh, as color drained from the dusk of your face, the knot of the universe unraveled before you, you looked down on me, marveling at how it was just a matter of footprints. Heel. Instep. Ball. Toes. Ahead of you, something waited, hand outstretched, ready to lead you into the pines. Show you that place where hosts of blueberries sing hosannas in the ferns and sand.

Bigfoot Gives Thanks

after Gerard Manley Hopkins

He doesn't chase down a turkey, wring
its pink neck like a wet dish rag,
gut it with his thumb, cook it
in sun with fly and maggot for days,
serve sides of chewed yam,
moose marrow, fermented pumpkin
guts, green with time, smelling
strong as a bear den at winter's end.
He doesn't smooth his hair with mud,
brush his teeth with fresh milkweed,
cram himself into a church pew
beside blue-haired widows who look
at his gorilla arms and long
to feel their dead husbands' dark
embraces at night again.
Doesn't stand when the organ
starts breathing music, raise the siren
of his voice to "Now Thank We
All Our God" until the stained glass
rattles and fractures.

No. His way is simpler. A morning
glory leaning toward day, unfolding,
shaking off the teary dew of darkness.
Stand outside at dawn. The bent
world is charged with his hairy
gratitude, in the long-legged shadows
of first and last light as they stretch
and stretch and stretch down the street,
across railroad trestle, through hayfields,
cornfields, into pines and poplar—
further and further—mountain,
swamp and lake, canyon and cave,
ocean, glacier, savanna, desert,
until, at last, they have touched
all the grandeur of deep down things.

    a bigfoot bestiary and other wonders

Bigfoot Blessing

May sun melt March frost on your body,
    make you spark and flash with dew.
May you sing as deep alders
    shimmy, a bald eagle takes wing.
May a bull moose scratch your back
    with its palmate antlers.
May your lice be few,
    your grubs plentiful,
your scat be soft,
    without bones.
May June rain brush the gnats
    out of your gums.
May barn owl not talon away
    your pet vole,
wolf and coyote not gnaw
    your dead father's ulna.
May you get drunk
    on raspberry ferment and mushroom.
May a sweet worm surprise
    the middle of your crabapple.
May you smell salmon dancing
    upstream for the drop of delicious salty roe.
May you find roadkill doe
    for a midnight snack.
May you press your tongue to love's
    hairy thigh under a breast of moon.
May autumn molt your coat
    to mustard and cranberry and squash,
fill your rooted cave
    with ripe plum, skunk scent.
May your sister's furred ghost crater
    the creek mud with footprints,
shiver midnight branches
    with her yawp and howl.
May December calm your restless fingers
    with snow and snow and snow.

Bigfoot Valediction

for Brianna, May 27, 2022

He is all goodbye, a dark palm
waving from the window of woods
on his way to some other place
where morels blossom like hairs
on his shoulders and porcupines gnaw
birch bark to paste. He is all letting
go of summer into harvest,
harvest into hibernation, the thunder
of his snores splitting cold nights
like a sharp tooth on the tongue
where the names of dead
grandmothers and lost friends
sit. He is not the fixed foot
of the compass, solid as mother
or father, but the wandering
foot of child, ever circling
wider and wider to find,
define its own circumference.
As you follow him tonight,
sweet girl, into the swamps
of frog song and mosquito sting,
remember to pause every then
and now, pick up a fallen
branch, and knock hard
on a cypress trunk. To let us
know you are alright. To remind
yourself of that nest of woolly
love you were born to leave.

Acknowledgments

Some of the poems in this book appeared, in earlier versions and/or with alternate titles, in the following:

Christmas with Bigfoot (Audio Album; Ronnie Ferguson, producer; Harvard Square Press): "Bigfoot Noel" (an earlier version of "Gaudete").

Jazzing with Bigfoot (Audio Album; Ronnie Ferguson, producer; Harvard Square Press): "The Eighth Day, a Bigfoot Creation Story," "Whitman and the Skunk," "White-tailed Deer and Lady Bigfoot on the Banks of Whitefish River, Lake Superior Region, Michigan, 1903. Photograph by George Shiras," "Pablo Auditions Bigfoot to Replace the Minotaur," "Frost and Bigfoot Duet in the Great Dismal Swamp," "Koi," "Bigfoot Gets Mistaken for John the Baptist at the Church of Corpus Christi," "Spring Choirs," "Bigfoot Crossing," "Bigfoot Visits My Father's Grave," "Bigfoot and Bird Celebrate Mardi Gras," "Bigfoot New Year's Resolution," "There is This," "Bigfoot Blessing," and "Doe After a Blizzard."

Slow Dancing with Bigfoot (Audio Album; Ronnie Ferguson, producer; Harvard Square Press): "Thirteen Ways of Looking at Bigfoot," "Bigfoot Takes His Wife to Mount Rushmore for Their Honeymoon," "A Pig's Orgasm Last 30 Minutes," "Lady Bigfoot Kept Him in Her Cave," "Bigfoot's Heart," "Butterflies Taste with Their Feet," "Bigfoot and Jim Harrison Skinny Dip in Morgan Pond on Father's Day," "Bigfoot Tries to Fix His Daughter's Broken Heart," "Bigfoot Meets a Homeless Man on Presque Isle," "Catfish Have 27,000 Taste Buds," "Slow Dancing with Bigfoot in Greenwich," "Starfish Have No Brains," "Ode to Kurt's Ashes in McLane Creek," "Elephants Are the Only Animals that Cannot Jump or, an Elephant Leap of Faith," and "Bigfoot Gives Thanks."

Superior Voyage: The Ten Year Anthology (Richard J. Rastall, editor; Gordon Publications): "Bigfoot Meets a Homeless Man on Presque Isle" and "Doe After a Blizzard."

The Way North: Collected Upper Peninsula New Works (Ron Riekki, editor; Wayne State University Press): "The Ugliest Fish in North America."

Yooper Poetry: On Experiencing Michigan's Upper Peninsula (Raymond Luczak, editor; Modern History Press): "Bigfoot and Jim Harrison Skinny-Dip in Morgan Pond on Father's Day," "Bigfoot's New Year's Resolutions," "Bigfoot Meets a Homeless Man on Presque Isle," "Portrait of the Virgin Mary as Skunk," and "Doe After a Blizzard."

The last line of "Stealing a Last Line from Keith Taylor" appears in the poem "From the Bluff" from Taylor's collection *Let Them Be Left: Isle Royale Poems*.

a bigfoot bestiary and other wonders

In Gratitude

I would like to thank the following individuals who have assisted me in chasing Bigfoot for the last 15 or so years: Janeen Rastall, whose ears and eyes made these pages sing in so many ways; Gala Malherbe, who helps me hear birds even in the dead of winter; B. G. Bradley, poet brother, who frequently reminds me that I'm so much bigger than Bigfoot; Beverly Matherne, mentor and friend, who lured me to the dark side; Ronnie Ferguson, who has partnered with me in hunting Bigfoot and so much more; members of the Marquette Poets Circle, who embrace and teach me about wonder every day; Jody Trost, who has always believed in Bigfoot and me, even when I didn't; my extended family, who never forced me to be anything other than my Bigfoot self; Amelia Pruiett, artist friend, who got my vision of Bigfoot and made it real; Raymond Luczak, editor and magician, who forced Bigfoot out of the woods; and Victor R. Volkman and Modern History Press, who gave Bigfoot a home. For those I lost along the way: my parents, Fred and Betty Achatz; brother, Kevin Achatz; sisters, Sally and Rosemarie Achatz; and friend in joy, Helen Haskell Remien. I know they are all slow dancing with Bigfoot right now. Finally and always, my wife, Beth, who fills my life with the greatest mystery—love.

About the Author

Martin Achatz grew up about 20 miles from the shores of Lake Superior in the Upper Peninsula of Michigan. He holds a BA in English, Computer Science, and Math; Master's in Fiction; and MFA in Poetry. For over 25 years, he has been a Contingent Professor for Northern Michigan University's English Department. After a long career in the healthcare industry, Achatz is currently the Adult Programming Coordinator for Peter White Public Library in Marquette, Michigan, hosting poetry readings, concerts, and cultural events, including two NEA Big Reads. In 2022, he helped establish the Great Lakes Poetry Festival.

Achatz's poetry and prose have appeared in *Kennesaw Review, The Paterson Literary Review, Dunes Review, The MacGuffin*, biostories.com, and elsewhere. Mayapple Press published his first collection of poems, *The Mysteries of the Rosary*, and his work has also appeared in numerous anthologies. Achatz has twice been nominated for the Pushcart Prize and worked as Poetry Editor for *Passages North* literary magazine. For two consecutive terms (2017-2020), Achatz served as U.P. Poet Laureate. For his accomplishments, the City of Marquette has awarded him Arts Advocate of the Year (2021) and Writer of the Year (2023). He is the current President of the U.P. Poet Laureate Foundation.

Achatz lives in Ishpeming, Michigan, with his family, and, in his spare time, chases comets and Bigfoot.

The anthology that sparked the Yooper Poetry Series!

Sometimes the best way to learn about a unique region is to listen to the stories told by those who've actually lived there. You learn things that no guidebook would ever tell you. You meet unforgettable characters who've strayed far off the beaten path. And you see clearly again how the power of memory is so strong that they can still recall incidents decades later. Michigan's Upper Peninsula has always been filled with remarkable sensations and indelible stories.

With this anthology, the editor Raymond Luczak sought to include poets who not only live in the U.P., but also who used to live there. What did it mean to be a Yooper then? What about now? Even for those who no longer abide there, the U.P. is indeed a special place, and it isn't just thanks to Mother Nature. The Yooper mindset requires a particular kind of faith in resilience against persistent odds.

The poets in this collection have never forgotten what it means to be a Yooper. Come partake in our celebration!

Martin Achatz | Jennifer Elen Bríd | B. Harlan Deemer | Chad Faries
Deborah K. Frontiera | Kathleen M. Heideman | John Hilden
Jonathan Johnson | Kathleen Carlton Johnson | Ellen Lord | Raymond Luczak
Gala Malherbe | Beverly Matherne | R. H. Miller | Jane Piirto | Dana Richter
T. Kilgore Splake | Suzanne Sunshower | Russell Thorburn

ISBN: 978-1-61599-793-0

Available in paperback, hardcover, ebook, and audiobook
Available via Modern History Press
modernhistorypress.com/YPS